PIG DREAMS

PIG DREAMS

Scenes from the Life of Sylvia

Poems by

DENISE LEVERTOV

Pastels by

LIEBE COOLIDGE

THE COUNTRYMAN PRESS

WOODSTOCK · VERMONT

Design and production by Guy Russell
Duotones and separations by Carl Sesto
Typeset by Monotype Composition Co.
Bound by the New Hampshire Bindery

Library of Congress Cataloging in Publication Data
Levertov, Denise, 1923–
    Pig dreams.
    Summary: A collection of seventeen poems about
Sylvia, a Vermont-bred pig.
    1. Swine—Poetry. [1. Pigs—Poetry. 2. American
poetry]   I. Coolidge, Liebe, ill.   II. Title.
PS3562.E8876P5   811'.54   81-9700
ISBN 0-914378-82-1   AACR2
ISBN 0-914378-83-X (signed lim. ed.)

Contents

To Sarah, Sylvia, and Ira

Her Destiny

The beginning: piglet among piglets,
the soft mud caking
our mother's teats.
Sweetsqueal, grunt:
her stiff white lashes, the sleepy
glint of her precious
tiny eyes.

*

But I am Sylvia. Chosen.
I was established
pet. To be
the pig of dreams, the pig
any of us could be,
       taken out of the sty,
       away from the ravaged soil of pig-yards,
       freed from boredom and ugliness.
I was chosen to live without dread of slaughter.

*

For three days, after they took me,
I hungered. Nowhere a teat to suck from,
no piglet siblings to jostle and nudge.
At last
    in the full moon's sacred light
    in the human room where I'd run
    in circles till my tapping trotters
    almost gave way,

the He-human
            naked and white as my
            lost mother,
bent on all-fours over my untouched bowl,
his beard a veil before me,
and with musical loud sounds of guzzling
showed me *eating*. Gave me
the joy of survival.

                        *

Quicklearner, soon
I could hold my shit.
I was rocked in warm
human arms.
I liked laps, the thighs
of humans.
Cuddling.
            Every pig
could be cuddled if there were justice.
            Every human
could have its intelligent pig,
            every pig
its dextrous human. Our lives
would be rich as creamy corn,
tasty as acorns.

Dogbrothers

Pigalone. Sylvia.
Sylvia Orphan Onlypig.
Even my She-human's lap
could not console.
But then I found
my Dogbrothers.
Bark and growl,
dog-laugh, waving
tails and the joy
of chasing, of whirling,
squealing, my dainty trotters
trilling beneath me
sharp and sure!
Of huddling to doze
in warm quickbreathing
muddle of dogs,
almost believing
I, Sylvia,
am dog not pig.

The Catpig

John the Cat
is most my brother,
almost pig

even though he
leaps among branches,
climbs to high shelves,
is silky.

Black and white Catpig,
I outgrew you,
but once we matched.

She-human gave us
our milk from
our pitcher.

Quiet we sat
under the sumacs of Vermont
and watched

the birds leave,
the first snow
pepper each other's
somber faces.

Winterpig

At the quick of winter
moonbrightest
snowdeepest

we would set out.
I'd run up my ramp
into the pickup,

we'd rattle and shake
two midnight miles
to the right hill.

Then on foot,
slither and struggle
up it—

they'd
ready their sled
and toboggan down

and I'd
put down my nose and
spread my ears and

tear down beside them,
fountains of snow
spurting around me:

I and my Humans
shouting, grunting,
the three of us

wild with joy,
just missing
the huge maples.

Yes, over and over
up to the top of the
diamond hill—

the leanest, the fastest,
most snow-and-moon-and-midnight-bewitched
pig in the world!

The Bride

They sent me away to be bred.
I was afraid, going down the ramp
from the truck to the strange barn,
I tried to run for the farmyard—strangers
shouted, they drove me inside.

In the barn a beautiful, imperious boar
dwelt in majesty. They brought me to him.
In the hot smell of him, I who was delicate,
       Sylvia the pet,
               who smelled of
       acorns and the windscoured pasture,
     I, Sylvia the Dreamer,
was brought low,
was brought
into the depths
of desire.
       I steeped my soul
               in the sweet dirt,
             the stench of
     My Lord Boar.

         *

Terrible, after the sensuous dark,
       the week of passion and feasting,
—terrible my return.
I screamed when they dragged me
outdoors to the truck. Harsh light
jumped at my eyes. My body's weight
sagged on my slender legs.

In the house of My Lord Boar
I had eaten rich swill.

Back home, I headed for my
private house, the house of Sylvia—
and my swill-swollen body
        would not enter,
        could not fit.

In shame I lay
many nights
on the ground outside my Humans' window
and passed my days silent and humble
in the bare pasture, until I was lean again,
            until I could enter
            my maiden chamber once more.

But now I carried in me
the fruit of my mating.

Her Task

My piglets cling to me,
perfect, quickbreathing, plump—
kernels of pearly sweetcorn,
milky with my milk.

These shall I housetrain, I swear it,
these shall dwell like their mother
among dextrous humans, to teach them
pig-wisdom. O Isis, bless
thy pig's piglets.

Her Secret

In the humans' house
fine things abound:
furniture, rugs by the hearth,
bowls and pitchers, freezer and fridge,
closets of food, baskets of apples,
the Musical Saw on which
my He-human plays
                    the songs I dream . . .

In my neat A-frame
they think there is nothing,
only the clean straw of my bed.
But under the floor I gather
beautiful tins, nutshells, ribbons,
shining buttons, the thousand baubles
a pig desires.

They are well hidden.
Piglets shall find one day
an inheritance of shapes,
textures, mysterious substances—

Rubber! Velvet! Aluminum! Paper!

Yes, I am founding,
     stick by stick,
     wrapper by wrapper,
     trinkets, toys—
Civilization!

Her Nightmare

The dream is blood: I swim,
which is forbidden to pigs,
and the doom comes: my sharp
flailing feet cut
into my thick throat
and the river water
is stained, and fills, and
thickens with bright blood
and darkens, and I'm
choking, drained,
too weak to heave
out of the sticky
crimson mud, and
I sink and sink in it
screaming, and then
voiceless, and
when I wake it's
the dark of the moon.

Yet, when I was young,
not knowing the prohibition,
I did swim. The corn
was tall, and my skin
was dry as old
parchment of husks,
the creviced earth
scorched, and no rain
had fallen
for long and long:
when my She-human plunged
into the lovely
cool and wet river,

I too
plunged, and swam.
It was easy to me
as if the water
were air, and I
a young bird in flight.
My pig-wings
flailed, but my throat
was not slit, and we crossed
the river, and rested
under splashed leaves
on the far shore,
and I thought I would always
be Sylvia Waterpig.
O it was sweet
to be upborne
on the fresh-running current,
a challenge to push
across it and gain
the moss and shade.
I escaped
the doom
then.
       But I grew
heavier, thick in the throat,
properly pigshaped,
and learned the Law.
And now,
this dream, on some
black nights, fills up
my bowl of sleep
with terror,
with blood.

Her Lament

When they caressed
and held in loving arms
the small pig that I was,
I was so glad, I blessed
my singular fate.
How could I know
my Humans would not grow
to fit me, as I became
Sylvia the Sow?
He-and-She-Human stayed the same, and now
even look smaller.
Perhaps I should not have learned
to adore
pleasures that could not last?
I grew so fast.
My destiny
kept me lean, and yet
my weight increased.
Great Sylvia, I must stay
under the table at the humans' feast.
And once, scratching my back on it,
I made the table fall
dishes and all!
How could a cherished piglet
have grown so tall?

Her Sadness

When days are short,
mountains already
white-headed, the west
red in its branchy
leafless nest, I know

more than a simple
sow should know.

I know
the days of a pig—
and the days of dogbrothers, catpigs,
cud-chewing cowfriends—
are numbered,

even the days of
Sylvia the Pet,

even the days
of humans are numbered.
Already

laps are denied me,
I cannot be cuddled,
they scratch my ears
as if I were anypig, fattening for bacon.

I shall grow heavier still,
even though I walk
for miles with my Humans,
through field and forest.

Mortality
weighs on my shoulders,
I know
too much about Time for a pig.

Her Sister

Kaya, my gentle
                Jersey cowfriend,
                                you are no pig,
you are slow to think,
                your moods
                                are like rounded clouds
drifting over the pasture,
                casting
                                pleasant shadows.
You lift your head
                slowly
                                up from the grass
to greet me.
                Occupied
                                with your cud, you are
all cow,
        yet we are friends,
                                or even sisters.
We worship
                the same goddess,
                                we look
to the same humans
                with love,
                                for love.
When I tread
                the mud in pigpatterns
                                after a shower,
my footprints shine
                and reflect the sky:
                                in this
they resemble your huge
                kindly eyes.
                                My own
are small,
        as befits a pig,
                                but I behold your steep
graygold side,
                a bulwark
                                beside me.

Pigsong

Walnut, hickory, beechmast.
apples and apples, a meadow
of applegrass dapple.
Walnut, hickory, beechmast.
And over the sunfall slope,
cool of the dark mudwallow.

Her Delight

I, Sylvia, tell you, my piglets:
it has been given me
to spend a whole day up to my snout
in the velvet wetness that is mud:

and to walk undriven, at dusk,
back to the human-house
and be welcomed there:

welcomed by humans and cats and dogs,
not reproached for my mantle
of graying mud:

welcomed, and given to eat
a food of human magic, resembling mud
and tasting
of bliss: and its holy name
is *chocolate.*

I, Sylvia, your mother,
have known
the grace of pigjoy.

Her Judgement

I love my own Humans and their friends,
but let it be said,
that my litters may heed it well,
their race is dangerous.

They mock the race of Swine, and call
"swinish" men they condemn.
Have they not appetites? Do *we*
plan for slaughter to fill our troughs?

Their fat ones, despised, waddle large-footed,
their thin ones hoard
inedible discs and scraps
called "money." Us they fatten,
us they exchange for this;

and they breed us not that our life
may be whole, pig-life
thriving alongside dog-life, bird-life,
grass-life, all
the lives of earth-creatures,

but that we may be devoured. Yet,
it's not being killed for food
destroys us. Other animals
hunt one another. But only Humans,

I think, first corrupt their prey
as we are corrupted, stuffed with temptation
until we can't move,

crowded until we turn on each other,
our name and nature abused.

It is their greed
overfattens us.
Dirt we lie in
is never unclean as their minds,
who take our deformed lives
without thought, without
respect for the Spirit Pig.

Her Vision

My human love, my She-human,
speaks to me in Piggish. She knows
my thoughts, she sees my emotions
flower and fade, fade and flower
as my destiny unrolls
its carpet, its ice and apples.

Not even she
knows all my dreams.
Under the russet sky
at dusk
I have seen
the Great Boar pass

invisible save to me.

His tusks are
flecked with skyfoam.
His eyes
red stars.

Her Prayer

O Isis my goddess,
my goddess Isis,
forget not thy pig.

Isis Speaks

Sylvia, my faithful
Petpig, teacher
of humans, fount
of pigwisdom:
you shall yet know
the grief of parting:
your humans, bowed with regret,
shall leave you.
But hear me,
this is no dream:
the time shall come
when you shall dwell,
revered,
in a house of your own
even finer than that you have.
And though you no longer
enter the houses of humans,
in springtimes to come
your black hide shall be strewn
with constellations of blossom.
Yes, in the deep summers,
apples shall bounce on your roof,
the ripe and round
fruit of your own appletree.
There you shall live long, and at peace,
redreaming the lore of your destiny.